a Gift from:
Mt. Washington Valley
Habitat for Humanity

RAISING THE ROOF

RAISING THE ROOF

Written by
RONALD KIDD

Illustrated by
JADA ROWLAND

A Habitat for Humanity Book

HABITAT FOR HUMANITY INTERNATIONAL

Americus, Georgia

To Ida Sue Kidd and Susie Loscutoff
—R.K.

In memory of my grandmother,
Anna Grant,
who made a house a home.
—J.R.

Published by Habitat for Humanity International
121 Habitat Street
Americus, Georgia 31709-3498
1-800-422-4828

Millard Fuller • *President and Founder*
Joy Highnote • *Director, Product Development*
Joseph Matthews • *Director, Communication Services*

Edited, designed, and manufactured by
The Children's Marketplace
A division of Southwestern/Great American, Inc.
2451 Atrium Way, Nashville, Tennessee 37214
1-800-358-0560

Dave Kempf • *Vice President, Executive Editor*
Mary Cummings • *Managing Editor*
Ronald Kidd • *Project Editor*
Bruce Gore • *Book Design*

But do not forget to do good and to share,
for with such sacrifices God is well pleased.

Hebrews 13:16

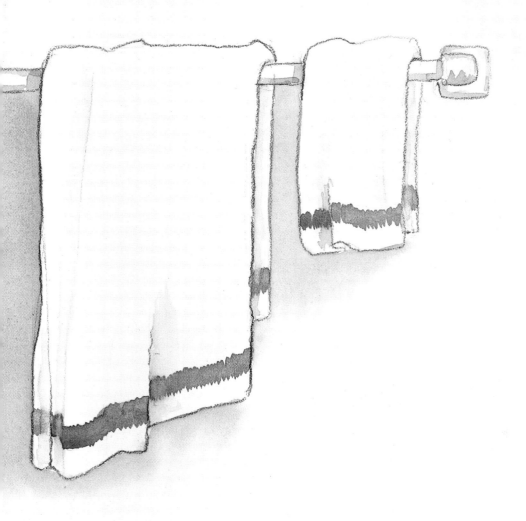

I like Monday.

That's the day when I help Dad get ready for work. If I'm good, he lets me put shaving cream on his face. If I'm really good, he lets me put it on mine.

I like Friday, too.

That's the day when Mom picks up ice cream on the way home. The ice cream makes me feel cold inside. Mom's smile makes me feel warm inside.

I like Saturday the best.

That's the day when I have Mom and Dad all to myself. We go to the park and play on the swings and have a picnic. It's just the three of us.

At least that's the way it used to be. Then one day it changed.

"David, we can't take you to the park today," said Mom one Saturday morning. "We're going to help build a house."

"Can I come with you?" I asked.

"I'm afraid not," Dad said. "It's only for grownups. While we're working, you can play with your friends at church."

They dropped me off at church. My friend Mrs. Green was there. But the two people I wanted most, my mom and dad, were gone.

In a corner of the yard was a big box.
I looked at it all morning, then asked Mrs.
Green if I could use it. She said yes and
helped me carry it out into the yard. Then
I got some scissors and went to work.

A girl came over and asked what I was making. I told her, "It's a house, like the one my mom and dad are building."

"Do you need any help?" she asked.

"No," I said. "This is my house."

She sat on a bench and watched me work. After a while she started wiggling around, as if she wanted to say something.

"Okay, what is it?" I asked her.

"I have an idea."

"I'm sorry," I said, "but I'm too busy."

Soon the house was finished, and I
crawled in. There was a knock at the door.
"Go away," I said.
"It's a really good idea," said the girl.
I didn't say anything.

That night, Mom and Dad told me
about the house they were building. It was
started by a group called Habitat for
Humanity. People from all over town
worked on it.

I told Mom and Dad about the house
I had made.

Dad said, "We're glad you had fun,
because we've decided to work on the
Habitat house again next Saturday."

"What about the park?" I asked.

"We'll go there pretty soon," he said.

Pretty soon seemed like a long time.

When Saturday came, Mom and Dad drove me to church again. But this time we went through a neighborhood I had never seen. We stopped in front of a little house.

Mom said, "This is where the Millers live."
"I think they need a new house," I said.
"That's what Habitat for Humanity thought," she told me.

We drove a little farther. Dad said, "This is the Habitat house we've been building. The Millers will move in as soon as it's finished."

A man saw us and waved.

"That's Mr. Miller," said Mom. "He's so excited about building his new home that he wants to work on other Habitat houses."

"Who are the other people?" I asked.

Mom said, "They're volunteers, like us. They don't get paid for their work. They're doing it because they want to help."

Dad said, "The man in the blue shirt is the project manager. He reads the plans. The woman next to him is a plumber. She puts in water pipes."

"What do you and Mom do?" I asked.
"I hammer, and she saws. Everybody's
good at something. That's why it takes
more than one person to build a house."

When they dropped me off at church, I noticed the girl from last Saturday.

"You know," I said, "it takes more than one person to build a house."

She nodded.

I said, "If you want to, you could tell me your idea now."

Her idea was to decorate the outside of the house. Some of her friends had more good ideas. By the end of the day, my plain house was a beautiful house.

That's when I had the best idea of all. I cut a hole in the roof and dropped a quarter inside.

"That's for Habitat for Humanity," I said, "so they can build more houses."

When our parents came to pick us up,
they put in money, too. We collected over
thirty dollars!

These days I still like Saturday the best.
That's the day when Mom and Dad
work with Habitat. Sometimes, after the
work is done, we look at houses and talk
about how they are made.

Dad says the best houses are the ones
you build together. I know he's right,
because my friends and I built one.
Someday we hope to build more.

RONALD KIDD is the author of thirty books for young readers and five plays. He received the Children's Choice Award and was nominated for the Edgar Allan Poe Award. Two of his plays were selected for development at the Eugene O'Neill Theater Center's National Playwrights Conference. He lives with his wife in Nashville, Tennessee.

JADA ROWLAND has illustrated many books for children, but is perhaps best known as an actress. She has performed both on stage and on television—for many years as Amy on *The Secret Storm* and as Carolee on *The Doctors*. Married to an astrophysicist, she makes her home in New York City.

Habitat for Humanity International
121 Habitat Street
Americus, Georgia 31709-3498

For more information, please call
1-800-HABITAT